COBRAS

John Willis

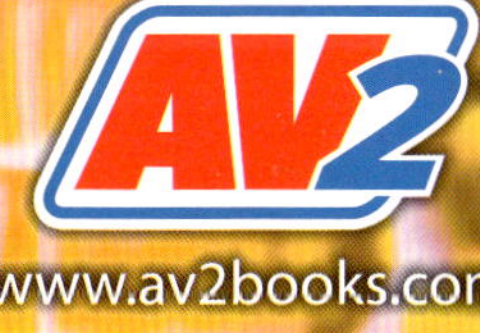

www.av2books.com

Step 1
Go to **www.av2books.com**

Step 2
Enter this unique code
ZKWYSE07I

Step 3
Explore your interactive eBook!

AV2 is optimized for use on any device

Your interactive eBook comes with...

Contents
Browse a live contents page to easily navigate through resources

Audio
Listen to sections of the book read aloud

Videos
Watch informative video clips

Weblinks
Gain additional information for research

Slideshows
View images and captions

Try This!
Complete activities and hands-on experiments

Key Words
Study vocabulary, and complete a matching word activity

Quizzes
Test your knowledge

Share
Share titles within your Learning Management System (LMS) or Library Circulation System

Citation
Create bibliographical references following the Chicago Manual of Style

This title is part of our AV2 digital subscription

1-Year 3–8 Subscription
ISBN 978-1-7911-3306-1

Access hundreds of AV2 titles with our digital subscription.
Sign up for a FREE trial at **www.av2books.com/trial**

COBRAS

CONTENTS

The Hooded Snake

Cobras are some of the best-known snakes on Earth. They are a group of snakes known for their powerful **venom** and the hoods on their necks. Their name comes from the Portuguese phrase *cobra de capello*, or "hooded snake." Cobras are part of the elapid **family** of snakes. This family also includes coral snakes and mambas. Elapids are usually slender snakes with venomous bites.

Like all other snakes, cobras are reptiles. This means that they have scaly bodies. They must use their surroundings to keep warm or to cool down.

SNAKE BITES

One king cobra bite has enough venom to kill **20 people**.

Some cobras can spit their venom more than **6.5 feet** (2 meters).

What Do Cobras Look Like?

Cobras usually have thin bodies. These snakes come in many different lengths. Most cobras are between 3 feet (0.9 m) and 7 feet (2.1 m) in length. King cobras are the largest venomous snakes on Earth. They can reach lengths of more than 18 feet (5.5 m).

Measuring Up

Average snake lengths

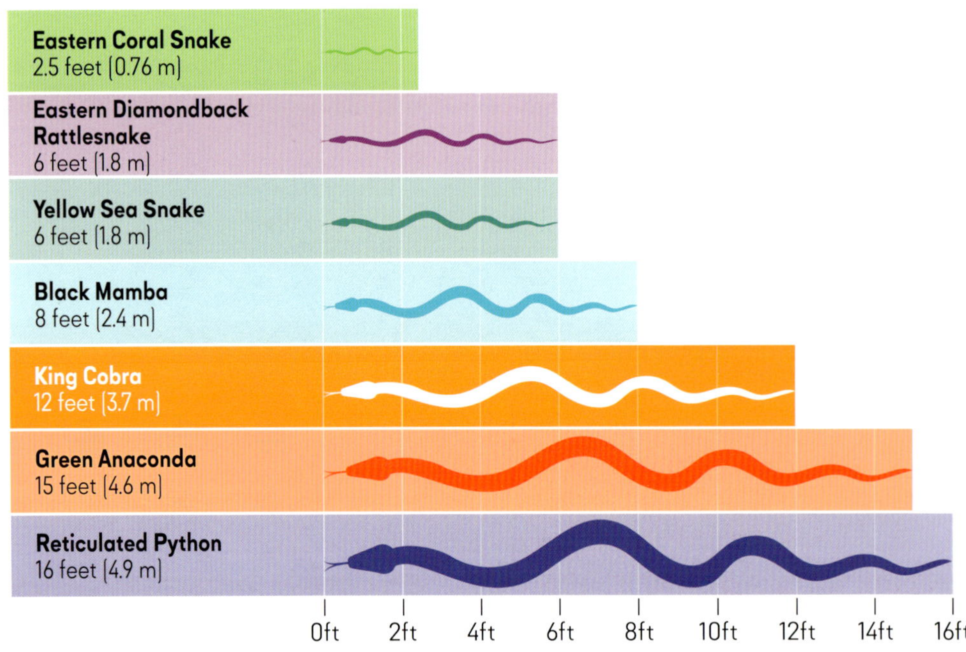

Cobras often have patterns on their hoods. In some **species**, such as the monocled cobra and the Indian cobra, these patterns look like eyes. They may help stop animals from attacking the snake from behind.

Cobras come in many different colors. These can include black, yellow, red, and white. Cobras may also have differently colored stripes or bands. Their bellies may be different colors from their backs.

The Life Cycle

Like all living things, cobras have a life cycle. A cobra will be born, grow, and **reproduce**. A cobra may live up to 30 years.

A cobra mother lays as many as 60 eggs. She guards them for up to 80 days until they are ready to hatch.

2
Baby cobras are called hatchlings. They are able to open their hoods and bite as soon as they are born.
3
A young cobra hunts and eats small animals. A cobra will often reach its adult size after 4 to 6 years.
4
Adult male cobras use their sense of smell to find a **mate**. Some males will dance to attract a mate. Others compete by wrestling with other males.

A Cobra's Body

Like all living things, a cobra has many different **adaptations**. Some keep the snake safe. Others help it to survive in its **habitat**.

Skin
Like all snakes, cobras shed their skin as they grow.

Tongue
Cobras have forked tongues. They use their tongues to pick up odors on the ground and smell them.

Hood
A cobra uses its neck muscles to spread out its ribs and stretch out its hood. This makes it look larger and more dangerous.

Fangs
Cobras have short **fangs**. This keeps the cobra from biting itself when it closes its mouth.

Where Cobras Live

Cobras are mostly found in **tropical** climates. They live in Africa and Southeast Asia. Cobras are often found in rainforests, grasslands, woodlands, deserts, and wetlands.

Cobra Range

Africa
Asia

Cobra Habitats

Desert
Forest
Grassland
Rainforest
Wetland

King Cobra

The king cobra is not a "true" cobra. It is larger and has a narrower hood. King cobras are found throughout Southeast Asia, including northern India. They get their name because much of their diet is made up of other snakes.

Mozambique Spitting Cobra

This snake is one of the most common cobras found in southern African countries such as Mozambique. Mozambique spitting cobras are responsible for more dangerous bites in southern Africa than any other snake.

Egypt

Egyptian Cobra

The Egyptian cobra is a large snake found in northern African countries, including Egypt. This snake was often used as a symbol in ancient Egyptian art. Egyptian cobras often encounter people when the snakes hunt small animals in and around farms.

On the Hunt

Most cobras spend their days resting. They typically hunt during dusk and dawn. Cobras find **prey** using their senses of smell and sight. They can see well in the dark. Cobras mostly eat small animals such as rodents, birds, lizards, and other snakes.

After a large meal, a cobra can go for months without eating.

Cobras use their venomous bites to hunt. Once a cobra finds its prey, it strikes using its fangs. Cobras may strike their food more than once because they have small fangs.

Cobras swallow their meals whole.

Keeping Safe

Although cobras have powerful venom, they are not typically **aggressive** snakes. When threatened, a cobra will often try to flee. If a cobra cannot run away, it will raise the top third of its body, spread its hood, and hiss. This will often chase away **predators**.

Spitting cobras have openings in the front of their fangs. By squeezing venom **glands** in their bodies, they spray venom from these openings.

Mongooses often hunt cobras. Their thick fur and fast speed helps them avoid being bitten.

Spitting cobras aim for the eyes of predators. Their venom can cause blindness.

Threats to Cobras

Today, cobras face several threats to their survival. Although most cobras are not **endangered**, many are decreasing in number every year. The king cobra, Chinese cobra, and black and white spitting cobra are all considered to be **vulnerable**.

The number of Chinese cobras has dropped 30 to 50 percent during the last 20 years.

Habitat loss is one of the major threats facing cobras today. As people cut down forests for lumber or make grasslands into farms, animals such as cobras lose the space they need to live. This also leads to more people encountering and possibly being bitten by cobras.

People also hunt cobras. Some are hunted for their meat or skin. Others are killed because people are afraid of them. In many countries, such as India, threatened cobras are now protected by law.

King cobra numbers have fallen more in some countries than in others. Today, these snakes are common in Thailand but scarce in China.

SNAKE BITES

The king cobra was declared a vulnerable species **in 2010**.

More than **50,000 people** in India died from snake bites each year between 2000 and 2019.

ACTIVITY

Create a Snake

There are many different kinds of snakes in the world. They all have certain features in common. However, each snake also has its own unique features. They help the snake live in its home.

Make your own snake by answering the following questions:

1. What is your snake called?
2. Where does it live?
3. What features does it share with other snakes?
4. What features help it live in its home? How do these features do this?
5. What does your snake look like?
6. Use a pencil or pen to draw your snake living in its home. Make sure to include all of its features.

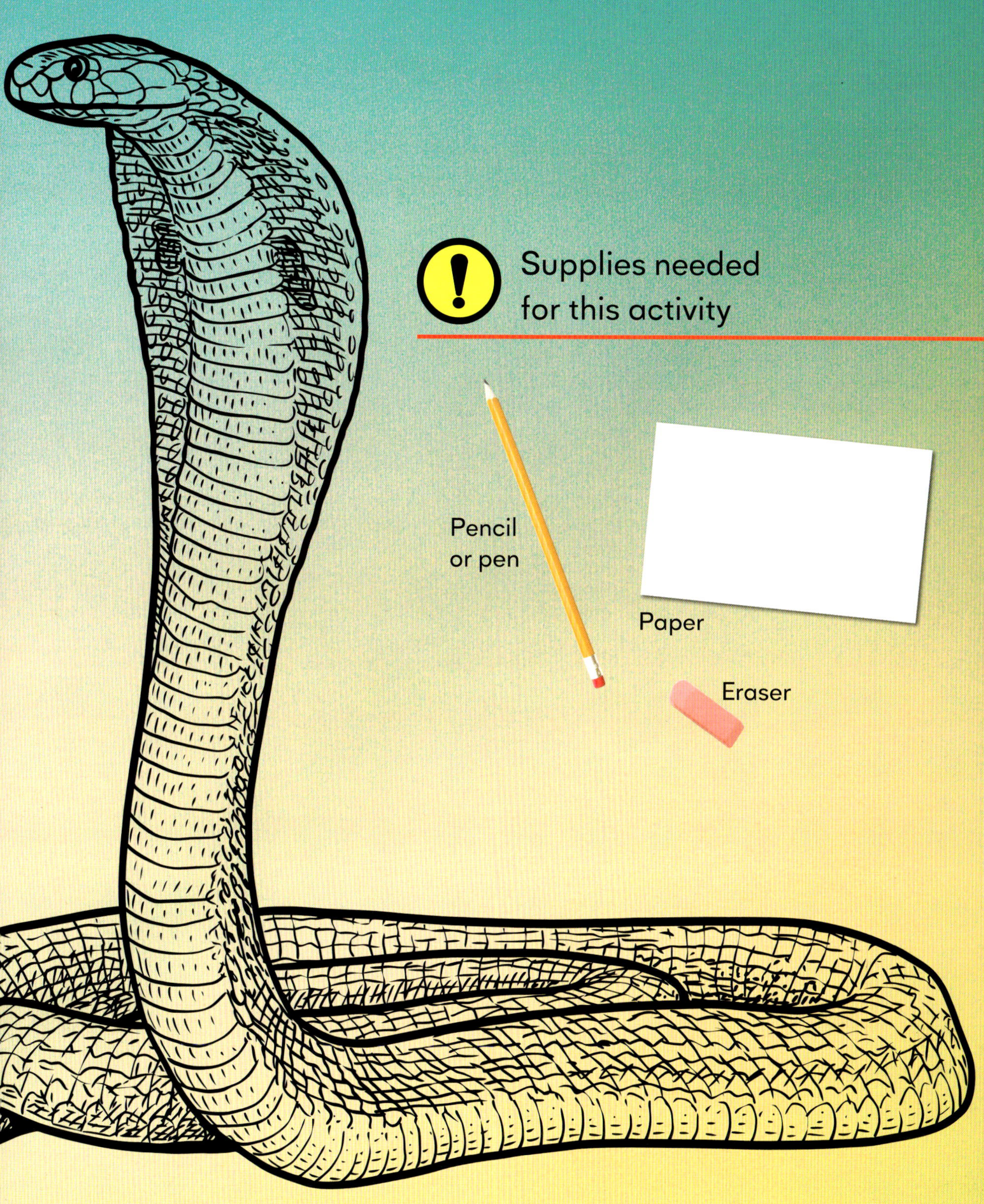
Supplies needed
for this activity
Pencil
or pen
Paper
Eraser

COBRA QUIZ

How well do you know your cobras? Take this short quiz to find out.

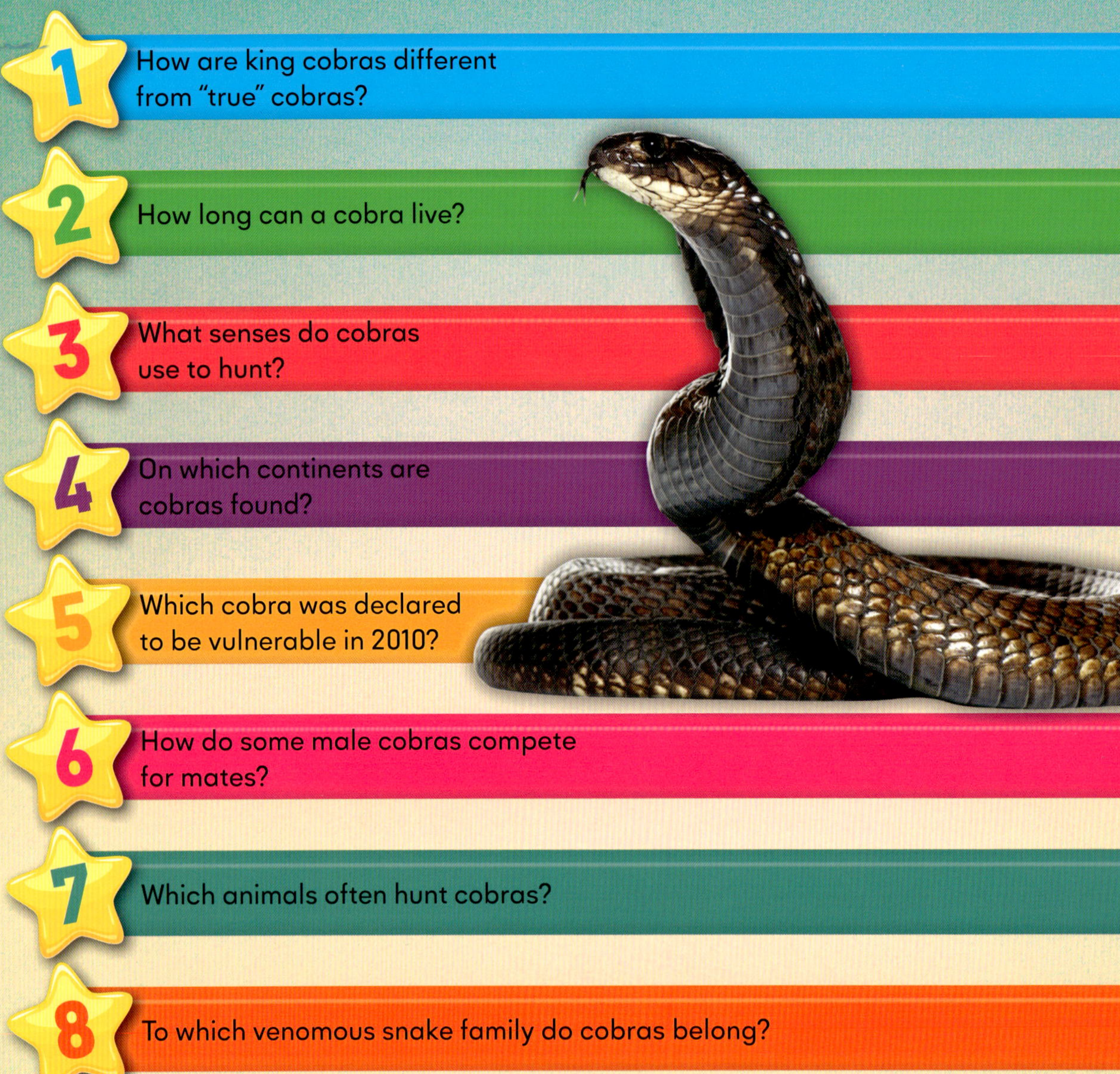

1. How are king cobras different from "true" cobras?
2. How long can a cobra live?
3. What senses do cobras use to hunt?
4. On which continents are cobras found?
5. Which cobra was declared to be vulnerable in 2010?
6. How do some male cobras compete for mates?
7. Which animals often hunt cobras?
8. To which venomous snake family do cobras belong?

ANSWERS

1. They are larger and have a narrower hood. **2.** Up to 30 years **3.** Sight and smell **4.** Africa and Asia **5.** The king cobra **6.** By dancing or wrestling **7.** Mongooses **8.** Elapid

Key Words

adaptations: changes in animals or plants that make them better able to survive in their homes

aggressive: ready to fight

endangered: close to becoming extinct

family: a group of living things that share certain characteristics

fangs: sharp, pointed teeth or similar parts of an animal's mouth

glands: parts of a body that produce substances it can use

habitat: the place where a plant or animal lives

mate: a member of a pair of animals that can reproduce, or have babies

predators: animals that hunt other animals

prey: animals that are hunted by other animals

reproduce: to have babies

species: a group of closely related animals or plants

tropical: places that are warm year-round

venom: a toxic chemical produced by some animals

vulnerable: likely to become endangered soon

Index

Get the best of both worlds.

AV2 bridges the gap between print and digital.

The expandable resources toolbar enables quick access to content including **videos**, **audio**, **activities**, **weblinks**, **slideshows**, **quizzes**, and **key words**.

Animated videos make static images come alive.

Resource icons on each page help readers to further **explore key concepts**.

Published by AV2
276 5th Avenue
Suite 704 #917
New York, NY 10001
Website: www.av2books.com

Library of Congress Control Number: 2021940112

ISBN 978-1-7911-4148-6 (hardcover)
ISBN 978-1-7911-4149-3 (softcover)
ISBN 978-1-7911-4150-9 (multi-user eBook)

Printed in Guangzhou, China
1 2 3 4 5 6 7 8 9 0 25 24 23 22 21

062021
101120

Art Director: Terry Paulhus Project Coordinator: John Willis

The publisher acknowledges Alamy, Getty Images, Minden Pictures, and Shutterstock as the primary image suppliers for this title.